HELP YOUR CHILD TO SUCCEED

The essential guide for parents

Bill Lucas and Alistair Smith

Family Learning

Acknowledgements

Thanks to my family – Mum, Dad, Henrietta and Thomas – for helping me to succeed and for giving me so many great ideas, and to my wonderful former colleagues at the *Campaign for Learning* for their inspirational thinking about family learning.

Bill Lucas

Thanks to my mum for helping this child to succeed, to Ani who helped me persist and to Peter Kindersley for the original opportunity. Nicola gave support and ideas, especially for reading and writing.

Alistair Smith

We should also like to thank all those who helped in the preparation of this book. Special thanks to Margaret Chamberlain and Ian Dicks for their lively illustrations, and to Bridget Gibbs, who provided us with unstinting expert advice and guidance.

Published by
Network Educational Press Ltd
PO Box 635
Stafford
ST16 1BF
www.networkpress.co.uk

© Bill Lucas and Alistair Smith 2002
ISBN 1 85539 111 2

Managing Editor: Bridget Gibbs
Design: Ian Dicks, Neil Hawkins
Illustrations: Margaret Chamberlain, Ian Dicks
Printed in Great Britain by
Technographic, Colchester, Essex.

CONTENTS

Every parent wants the best for their child.

We want our children to do well at school and to get a good job. We want them to be happy and to feel fulfilled. But sometimes we don't know how best to help them.

This book has been written to support you in giving your child the help she needs – to show that you can make an enormous difference to your child's chances of success in life. It also shows how families can enjoy learning together. The home and its immediate environment offer wonderful opportunities for discovery, exploration, play, education and learning. Whether your child is an energetic pre-schooler, is just finding his feet in the early years at school, or is nearing the end of primary school, this book will help. Packed with activities, games and tips, together with suggestions for dealing with everyday concerns, such as helping with homework and things to do in the school holidays, it is both a practical reference guide for dipping into and a thought-provoking read.

Each chapter opens with a number of questions that introduce the topics it covers, followed by a fun quiz. A Quick Check summary at the end of each chapter acts as a reminder of the key points. Family games and information about using the internet are included in the Resources section at the back of the book. There is a list of useful websites for both you and your child – those that link specifically to topics in the book are indicated by the symbol **W** and listed by page number. For these, you will find **W** on the relevant pages throughout the book.

Lastly, we have sometimes used 'he' and sometimes 'she' throughout the book, but most of what we have to say applies equally to boys and girls. Every child deserves a good start in life – we hope this book goes some way towards helping you achieve this.

Alistair and Bill

It Starts With You!

Being your child's first teacher

Have you ever wondered...

? **Why you enjoy learning some things but not others?**

? **How to help your child to do well at the things you find difficult?**

? **How you can give your child the best possible start in life?**

? **How to make more time to spend with your child?**

Trying some of the ideas in this chapter will help you explore these issues.

You have the most important role to play in helping your child to succeed. Parents are a child's first teacher, and you can teach her how to learn. However, to help your child learn, you need to be a learner yourself.

? Did you know that your attitude to learning is the strongest influence on how successful a learner your child becomes?

WHAT DO YOU THINK ABOUT LEARNING?

	Yourself		Your partner	
	Yes	No	Yes	No
Did you enjoy primary school?	☐	☐	☐	☐
Did you enjoy secondary school?	☐	☐	☐	☐
Do you enjoy learning new things?	☐	☐	☐	☐
Do you ever worry you will look foolish?	☐	☐	☐	☐
Do you know what distracts you?	☐	☐	☐	☐
Is learning important in your life?	☐	☐	☐	☐
Would you make a good teacher?	☐	☐	☐	☐
Do you know how you learn best?	☐	☐	☐	☐

HOW DO YOU PREFER TO LEARN?

	Yes	No	Yes	No
By doing practical things?	☐	☐	☐	☐
On your own?	☐	☐	☐	☐
In a group?	☐	☐	☐	☐
By talking?	☐	☐	☐	☐
By watching?	☐	☐	☐	☐
By listening?	☐	☐	☐	☐
By copying an 'expert'?	☐	☐	☐	☐
By thinking things through for yourself?	☐	☐	☐	☐
With a friend or a coach?	☐	☐	☐	☐

WHICH OF THESE METHODS DO YOU PREFER?

Books?	☐	☐
Videos?	☐	☐
TV programmes?	☐	☐
CD/computers?	☐	☐
Internet?	☐	☐

Discuss your answers with your partner or a friend:

- Are they similar or different?
- If your school days were not happy, how do you think this might influence you when thinking about your child's school?
- Do you think you learn in similar ways to your children?
- Is there any aspect of you as a learner which concerns you? If so, share it!

Belonging Aspirations Safety Identity Challenge Success

Providing the BASICS

How a child feels about herself affects her approach to life. It influences her willingness to 'have a go' and take risks. It's difficult to say 'I don't know' or 'I need help' if you believe you're not good enough. It's more difficult to be successful if you don't think well of yourself.

Here are the elements of what we call the BASICS. They are key to effective family learning and developing your child's self-esteem.

Belonging

Everyone needs to feel they belong. Children need to feel valued and loved, both at home and at school. Make time to be with your child and listen to her. But there is more to it than just showing you care. If you establish routines for times like meals, baths, reading and bed, your child will know how you expect her to behave. This will help her to feel a sense of security and belonging.

Children with a strong sense of belonging are more likely to make friends who have similar clear guidance from their families. They will be more trusting in making friendships and less likely to be shy.

Did you know that if your child has low self-esteem, it's like driving through life with the handbrake on?

PAUSE FOR THOUGHT: Agreeing family mealtime rules

What do you expect from your children at meal times?
Try to agree some family mealtime rules. There are no right or wrong answers, but it helps to be consistent.

Aspirations

Aspirations are dreams about what's possible. We all have them, we all need them, but we seldom share them! Talk to your child about what's possible. Have positive aspirations of your own and share them with him.

If children want something, then they will really try to get it! They need to learn that to turn dreams into reality, they may have to alter or improve what they are doing. Sometimes, especially with younger children, this will involve you in saving rewards or treats until another day.

Once your child learns how to stick with things over time, his aspirations start to become his goals, for a goal is a dream with a timescale. Children who can set goals, and who work towards achieving those goals, will be more successful in later life.

Tips for developing your child's aspirational thinking

- Be positive. Turn 'can'ts' into 'cans'.
- Practise goal-setting in and around the home. Help your child set little targets and then discuss what she will have to do to achieve them. Catch her when she succeeds, and be there to support her if she fails!
- Share your own aspirations, 'I'm really looking forward to…'

ACTIVITY: Make an 'in my dreams' collage

1. You will need several magazines, scissors, glue and a large piece of paper.
2. Look through the magazines together and ask your child, 'What can you see here that you would like to do?'
3. Cut out the pictures that show the kind of things she wants to do.
4. Lay the pictures out on the paper to make a collage of her dreams.

Safety

Learning is risky, because of the possibility of failure. As a result, safety is very important. If your child is afraid of being put-down or hurt, he will try to avoid learning new things. Make sure when you do something together that you always remind him that it's okay to make mistakes.

Tips for developing your child's feelings of safety

- Apply the 4:1 rule: four positive comments for any negative one.
- Avoid any sort of put-down.
- Be consistent in how you use rules and always explain them clearly.

Identity

Your child is an individual. Allow her to follow her own interests and not just to copy yours! By learning about her own strengths and weaknesses, and what is important to her, your child is developing a sense of identity. Children with a strong sense of who they are, are often resilient and have more confidence. They learn and achieve more.

Tips for developing your child's identity

- Encourage your child to talk about feelings. This is particularly important for boys, who tend not to express themselves so freely.
- Share your own interests and enthusiasms. Take an interest in your child's, avoiding comparisons with others in the family unless you can do this in a positive way.

PAUSE FOR THOUGHT: Learning to express feelings

Think of a situation where your child bottled up her feelings. To help her express what she was feeling, draw a really simple picture about the occasion. Add speech bubbles that say what she was feeling, and then talk it through.

Challenge

We all need challenge (see chapter 2 for more on this). Our brains enjoy challenge but not so much of it that it becomes a threat. Children learn best from slightly difficult tasks that they have to work at.

Dealing with everyday challenges helps your child develop coping strategies. You will not be helping your child if you protect her in a cotton wool world. Instead, help her to learn the skills of coping, then next time a crisis occurs, she will have ways of dealing with it.

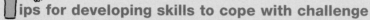

Tips for developing skills to cope with challenge

- Don't rush to help when your child struggles with an activity. Encourage her to keep trying.
- Break tasks down into smaller chunks that can be tackled one at a time.
- Help your child understand that mistakes are alright provided we learn from them. Learning is a messy business!

Boys and girls may learn to deal with everyday challenges in different ways.

ACTIVITY: Make a spider diagram

Use this when your child is struggling with something, and needs help to break the task down into more manageable chunks.

1. Write a brief description of the task in the middle of a large piece of paper.
2. Draw a circle around it.
3. Talk about how you could break the task down into a number of stages that seem more achievable.
4. Draw lines out from the circle, and write one stage down at the end of each line.
5. See if you can put what you have learned into practice.

Success

Success breeds success and failure breeds failure. But what does this mean? If children's small successes pass without comment, over time they can begin to believe they are 'not good at anything'.

Replace the concept of failure with feedback. Help your child to see mistakes as part of the process of learning. Make sure that she is also experiencing success. When she is doing something well, comment on it.

Tips for developing success in your child

- Comment positively on everyday successes using a success vocabulary: 'Well done for...', 'You did that well', 'Thank you for...'
- Encourage your child to notice when he improves on his personal best.
- Look on any failure as an opportunity to find out what went wrong and work out what to do better next time.

> It didn't work for us this time did it? let's try it another way shall we?

PAUSE FOR THOUGHT: Making a record of success

Make a 'Things I can do' folder or an 'I did this' board for your child. Include photos, certificates, letters, swimming badges or anything else that shows achievement. Encourage your child to show things she is proud of to her grandparents and to family friends.

Coaching Your Child

Coaching involves helping your child to find out how she is doing and what she can do to improve. Every parent can learn to be a coach, giving their child feedback as a natural part of daily life. Coaching will help to develop your child's self-esteem.

Focus on one issue at a time. For example, don't just say, 'Try to make your writing neater'; explain what you mean by 'neater' – such as, write on the lines, start on the left margin.

Focus on what your child is doing and don't start criticising her personality. Try to avoid saying, 'That's typical of you, Rachael, to be doing …' and instead say, 'Please put that down and let me show you how to…'

Timing is all-important. If your child is distressed, it is better to calm her down before attempting to give any advice.

Try to concentrate on one issue at a time, using the RESPECT method outlined below.

- **Reassuring:** 'I know you thought this would be a good way of doing this and…'
- **Enthusiastic:** 'I really liked the way you…'
- **Steady:** 'That's okay. I'll wait while you pick them all up again.
- **Practical:** 'Let's see what happens when we try this again. You stand over there and I'll...'
- **Engaging:** 'I'll do it first and then you try.'
- **Clear:** 'When you move your hand more slowly, you will stop smudging your writing.'
- **Truthful:** 'You're not as good at kicking with your left foot as your right, so we should practise…'

Asking the right questions and being a good listener are important in coaching. When your child has a problem or has difficulty with learning something, careful questions can help you both get to the heart of the matter and understand what the problem is.

Tips for asking questions and listening

- Make questions short, clear, constructive, and open-ended, so that you get a response other than just 'yes' or 'no'. Open questions start with Who, Where, What, When, Why or How.
- Don't jump in too early when your child is talking.
- Be ready to stop what you are doing to listen.

ACTIVITY: Practise your coaching skills

To be a good coach you don't necessarily have to be good at the activity you are coaching someone to do.

1. Get hold of some juggling balls.
2. Use the instructions that come with them to see how effectively you can help your partner or a friend learn to juggle.
3. Apply this to something you want to help your child with.

Making Time for Learning

Spending time with your children is one of the most important gifts you can give them. Try to have some time when you remove all disruptions and concentrate exclusively on your child. You might read a book together, visit a play area or fix a bicycle. This 'together time' is when you can shape attitudes and develop the kind of positive habits that encourage learning. **W**

Making time for learning is difficult. But it gets easier if you can establish patterns that work for you and your family. For example: 'We share meals and no-one watches television while we eat.' Does this sound impossible? The answer is that if you establish the pattern and stick to it, it becomes expected. Chapter 4 gives tips for making eating together fun.

Other examples of good patterns are:
- homework for twenty minutes before television;
- read together before bed.

Did you know that children spend less than 15% of their waking hours at school?

AUSE FOR THOUGHT: Together time

Together time works best when it happens regularly. Establish a slot, such as after supper or homework, when you and your child do things together. By sharing an activity regularly, you create a habit that can be looked forward to and talked about. Make sure you are free from distractions such as phones, TV and radio. Don't allow interruptions from others in the family.

Together time is best when you are both at your best. You may have rushed home from work or a late appointment for your Together time slot, but your child may be too tired. Don't go ahead at all costs, it may all end in tears. Save it for next time!

QUICK CHECK

✓ Remember that your attitude to learning is a major influence on your child's readiness to learn.
✓ Use the BASICS to improve your child's self-esteem: Belonging, Aspirations, Safety, Identity, Challenge and Success.
✓ Give specific and positive feedback to help your child improve.
✓ Spend quality time together with your child.

Your Child is a Learner

How you and your family can become learners

2

Have you ever wondered...

? What happens when you are learning?

? If there is a good way of learning?

? Whether play helps children to learn?

? What you can do to make your home a good place for learning?

Trying some of the ideas in this chapter will help you explore these issues.

The more you understand how you and your child learn, the better. By using some simple techniques, you can really help your child to get on.

? Did you know that laughing can help you to remember things?

HOW GOOD A LEARNER ARE YOU?

DO YOU...	Yourself		Your partner	
	Yes	No	Yes	No
1. Always have to get it right first time?				
2. Enjoy watching someone and copying them?				
3. Talk yourself through it?				
4. Try alternatives in your head?				
5. Do it again and again until you get better?				
6. Work out what you will do in detail beforehand?				
7. Ask lots of questions as you go?				
8. Give up easily?				
9. Set yourself a target or targets beforehand?				
10. Try to work out how it all fits together?				
11. Need to get up and move around a lot?				
12. Test yourself on what you have remembered?				

ANSWERS AND EXPLANATIONS

1. No. It can be helpful to experiment and try alternatives.

2. Yes. Imitating others is a great way to learn, it's how we learn to walk.

3. Yes. Talking aloud helps you to understand and remember.

4. Yes. Rehearsing in your head works!

5. Yes. Practice does make perfect!

6. Yes. Planning is an essential part of most successful learning.

7. Yes. Asking yourself questions is essential.

8. No. Staying positive and persisting is essential.

9. Yes. Setting goals helps you to stay motivated and purposeful.

10. Yes. Your mind loves to make connections and see patterns.

11. We are all different! Moving about may help to give you more energy.

12. Yes. Going over things on a regular basis helps. Little and often is best.

Discuss your answers to the questions and the explanations given alongside them. What might you do differently as a result?

Learning Through Play

Young children learn mainly through play. When they play, they experience rough and tumble. They rehearse, copy, tease, laugh and adapt. In play, a child pretends. So, for example, a child might blow on an empty toy cup, which contains imaginary coffee that is too hot.

Play is safe and doesn't threaten. It allows children to take risks. They can explore and be curious. They control and direct their own version of the world around them. Play is a great way to learn!

The best learning play occurs when you encourage:

Predicting   Exploring   Talking   Imagining   Practising

You can PDQ it!

Learning happens naturally through play. But you can support your child even more once you realise that most learning involves three stages. This is true whether you are just playing or involved in more structured learning.

The three stages are:
1. Getting yourself ready to learn
2. The learning itself
3. Checking that you have got it all worked out.
We call this PDQ.

PLAN FOR IT   **D**O IT   **Q**UIZ YOURSELF ABOUT IT

ACTIVITY: PDQ shopping with a young child

Plan for it

1. Talk to your child: 'We're going shopping today. What do we need?'
2. Make a list. Make sure you write clearly so that your child can read any words she knows and count the items with you.
3. Leave the big list at home to check things off when you get home, and write out a small list to take with you.

Do it

4. Set your child tasks at the supermarket: ask her to remember some things on the list; ask her to find specific items on the shelves.

Quiz yourselves about it

5. Talk to your child as you unpack the shopping.
6. Count out how many things you've bought and check them off against the big list you left at home.
7. Organise items into groups, ready to put away: things for the freezer, things for the fridge, tins and packets for the cupboard, and things for cleaning and the bathroom.

apples rice pasta fish fingers cheese carrots tea crisps washing up liquid tomatoes potatoes milk bread cake butter tooth-paste coffee

" When you learn something it lives inside your head forever. "

The Five Secrets

Things you can do to help your family learn more effectively are common sense. But they are rarely talked about, so we call them the five secrets.

1 Be positive and supportive

Your child will learn best when he feels able to take risks. Your expectations may make him anxious, so remember that being preoccupied with being the best and getting results may come at the expense of real learning. You can find out more about this in chapter 6.

Tips for creating a positive learning environment

- Avoid comparisons with other children.
- Avoid threats.
- Break learning up into small manageable chunks. Recognise each one as an achievement.

PAUSE FOR THOUGHT: Reflecting on your approach

Think of an activity you have done recently with your child. Ask yourself what specific things you did to keep him positive and free from anxiety.

2 Encourage planning and goal-setting

Start with the big picture. Before diving into any activity – a maths problem or finding out about something in history, for example – take time to get the overview. With young children, show how this helps by, for example, looking at the lid of a jigsaw puzzle or the instructions that go with a game.

Picture what success will be like before starting a task. How will children know they have achieved it? Take time to talk about this with your child.

Tips for looking ahead and setting goals

- Encourage your child to close his eyes and picture the task in his head. You may also want to suggest he thinks of people he knows who can do whatever it is he is planning.
- Ask questions that encourage looking ahead, such as: 'How long do you think this will take you?' and 'How will you know if you have learned these spellings?'
- Make a simple chart with your child that shows when he will do his homework and put it on his bedroom wall.

HOMEWORK	MON	TUES	WED	THUR	FRI
4.00	HOME-WORK	FOOT-BALL	CUBS	HOME-WORK	HOME-WORK
6.00	EAT	EAT	EAT	EAT	EAT
7.00	T.V	HOME-WORK	HOME-WORK	T.V	FOOT-BALL
8.30	BED	BED	BED	BED	BED

ACTIVITY: Planning homework

This big-picture approach to a history task can easily be adapted for other homework.

Suppose your child has to read a passage from a book about the Romans in Britain, then answer questions and draw an annotated cross-section of a Roman road. Before reading for information, he needs to get the 'big picture' by following the four steps below.

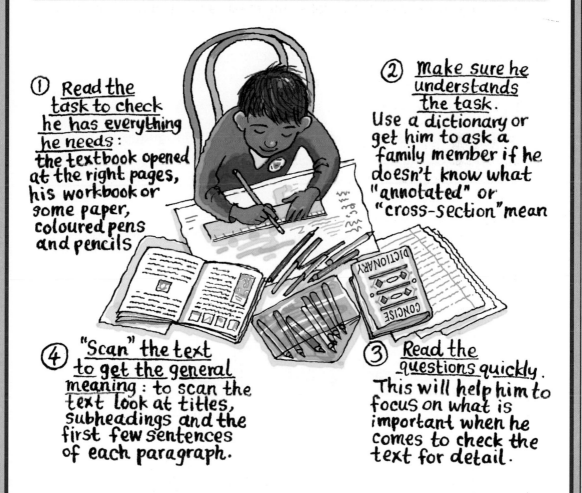

① Read the task to check he has everything he needs: the textbook opened at the right pages, his workbook or some paper, coloured pens and pencils

② Make sure he understands the task. Use a dictionary or get him to ask a family member if he doesn't know what "annotated" or "cross-section" mean

④ "Scan" the text to get the general meaning: to scan the text look at titles, subheadings and the first few sentences of each paragraph.

③ Read the questions quickly. This will help him to focus on what is important when he comes to check the text for detail.

Goal-setting

When your child has finished planning, help him to set targets and think about what success will feel like. In the activity above, his goals might be: 'I'll take 15 minutes to read the passage, then answer the first five questions, then take a break. I'll try and write at least three sentences for each answer. I'll finish this by 7.00pm and then do another 40 minutes tomorrow.' Ⓦ

3 Make connections with what your child already knows

We all find it easier to learn something new when we can connect it to something we already know. We need maps, lists and guides to help us make connections between things and then to see if there are any patterns to help us organise our thinking.

Tips for helping your child to make connections

- Encourage connections between words by asking your child questions like those in the picture below.
- Encourage your child to explain connections, both to herself as she works and to others.

PAUSE FOR THOUGHT: Accelerate your child's language learning

Your child's excitement at using language can take off when she learns a few simple connecting rules. For example, at some time she will find out that words can begin and end in similar ways – she is discovering prefixes and suffixes. Look at a junior dictionary and see how useful such connections and patterns are. For example, the prefix 'un' gives a word the opposite meaning, and new words can be made by adding 'ex' to the start of a word.

Gradually, you can go further. For example, 'bio' means 'life', and 'logy' means 'study of' – 'biology' means study of life; 'geo' means earth – 'geology' means study of the earth. And so on.

4 Help your child learn by seeing, hearing and doing

We continually get information through our senses. We store it, make connections and categorise it, and respond to it. Help your child learn through the senses and you will dramatically improve his chances of success.

Highly visual people remember what they see. They rehearse what things will look like in their head. They may spell by remembering the look of a word.

Some people use their eyes

People who depend on their ears rehearse what has been said to them over and over again. They may spell using patterns of sound, and often talk themselves through a process or a problem. They enjoy discussion.

People who use physical movement like to get up and get on with things. When they spell, they may use a finger to write in the air. They may need to write out a calculation to get the 'feel' of it. They learn best by experiencing things for themselves.

Some use their ears

Some use their bodies

Tips for learning by seeing, hearing and doing

- Encourage your child to put up posters around his room summarising what he needs to know. Give him bright coloured pens and large sheets of paper.
- Encourage him to listen to different types of music, and give him the option to have background music while he works.
- Give him lots of opportunities to dance and sing at an early age.

Did you know that every time you do something, thousands of nerve cells in your brain are connecting, and these connections are organised into patterns?

5 Use reviewing to help your child remember things

Regular review helps us to remember things. Encourage your child to pause frequently in what he is doing and take time to explain to himself what he has just learned. Time spent reviewing is time well spent.

PAUSE FOR THOUGHT: Using a multi-sensory approach

Think of something your child is currently trying to learn. Decide how you could help him, using three different ways: one focusing on eyes, one on ears, and one on the body and doing.

Tips to help your child review what he has learned

- Encourage your child to test himself regularly. Little and often is the key.
- Help him to practise talking himself through an activity aloud, looking at each step and saying what is involved. He will be using the language he needs, so he is more likely to remember it.
- Draw a poster or a mind map™ to help him remember something.

QUICK CHECK

✓ Be clear in your own mind about how children learn.
✓ Make sure your child learns PDQ (Plan, Do, Quiz).
✓ Remember the five things you can do to encourage effective learning.

3

Go For It!
Overcoming barriers to learning

Have you ever wondered...

? What effect stress has on learning?

? Why your child avoids doing certain things?

? How much pressure to put your child under?

? How to deal with your child's moods?

? About how friends can influence your children?

? What you can do to motivate your child?

Trying some of the ideas in this chapter will help you explore these issues.

Learning is not always easy. You often have to work hard. There are many ways in which you can help your child to stick with it.

Did you know that most barriers only exist inside our heads?

HOW DOES YOUR CHILD DEAL WITH DIFFICULTIES?

DOES HE/SHE.....	Never	Sometimes	Always
1. Get really frustrated and blame someone else?	☐	☐	☐
2. Try to avoid the difficulty by doing something else?	☐	☐	☐
3. Stay rooted to the spot not knowing what to do?	☐	☐	☐
4. Want to be with you or with her friends?	☐	☐	☐
5. Need you to make her try harder?	☐	☐	☐
6. Go into a sulk?	☐	☐	☐
7. Compare herself with her friends?	☐	☐	☐
8. Try harder?	☐	☐	☐

SOME EXPLANATIONS

1. Children often blame themselves or others if something seems too difficult, and this may lead to aggression or confrontation. This is called the 'fight' response.

2. 'Running away' is a frequent response to things that are difficult. This is called the 'flight' response.

3. The phrase 'getting stuck' says it all. Getting stuck is not a problem, but staying stuck is. Good learners are better at becoming unstuck. This response to anxiety is called the 'freeze' response.

4. Being with others who are like us helps us to cope with threat. This is called the 'flock' response.

5. Learning needs positive support and interest, but pushing your child too hard puts pressure on him and can be unhelpful.

6. We all react differently to situations, and your child's moods will fluctuate and change. When moods get linked to an experience – for example, if doing homework always causes a sulk – you need to help your child break the pattern.

7. Friends or 'peers' can exert a powerful influence. You need to keep watching and listening as peer pressure can be good or bad in learning.

8. 'Stickability' is the secret of success. So if 'try harder' means 'stick with it', that's good. But sometimes more of the same won't help – a different approach is needed.

> **If we could give a child one gift it would be to free them from a fear of failure.**

Recognising Barriers to Learning

Despite our natural curiosity, it's easy to get sidetracked from learning or to lose heart along the way. Here are just some of the likely barriers.

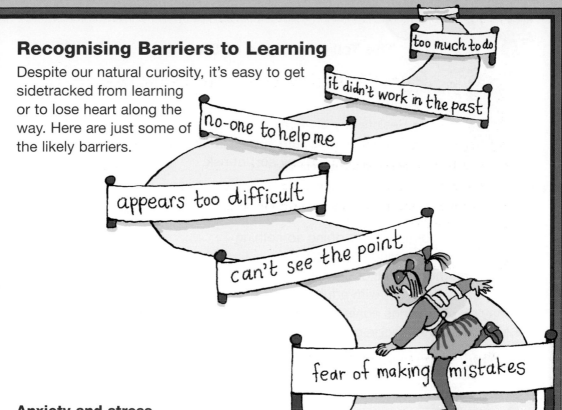

too much to do

it didn't work in the past

no-one to help me

appears too difficult

can't see the point

fear of making mistakes

Anxiety and stress

One of the main obstacles to learning is too much anxiety, which leads to stress. Your child will have the best chance to develop and grow if you can provide challenge together with support. But take care not to tip her into a situation where she feels vulnerable or threatened.

As far as the brain is concerned, there is no difference in the way it responds to a real threat and an imagined one. We deal with threats or difficulties in the four different ways shown below. How did you answer the first four quiz questions about your child's way of dealing with difficulties?

Fight   Flight   Freeze   Flock

The Tell-tale Signs of Stress

Fight behaviour
- Resists any change.
- Prefers what is safe and feels familiar.
- Unlikely to take any sort of risk.

Flight behaviour
- May avoid something by doing something else, even something she dislikes.
- May pretend to be ill or tired.
- Avoids eye contact with adults.
- May do safe things again and again.
- May stay on the edge of groups.

Freeze behaviour
- Unable to speak or do anything when she's put on the spot in some way.
- Goes blank when asked a question to which she knows the answer.

Flock behaviour
- Wants to be with friends.
- Wants to be like friends, not stand out in the crowd.
- Can lead to dumbing down: 'it's not cool to be keen'.

PAUSE FOR THOUGHT: Helping your child with stress

What makes your child stressed? Write a list of the situations. Now draw a chart like the one opposite. Write each situation in the box that matches your child's response to it. Think about what you could do to help him in each situation. Use the tips opposite to help you.

Tips for reducing your child's stress

- Find out where the threat, real or imagined, is coming from and help your child take steps to deal with it.
- Try to avoid showing your own anxieties. If you get agitated, your child may pick up on it. For example, if parents scream at spiders, their children often do too. But if they deal calmly with spiders, so do children.
- Encourage your child to make his own decisions, within limits that you set. This will help him to be confident in new situations. Talk through the pros and cons and the consequences of any choices.
- Try not to pressurise your child to get it right every time. If you do, he may not want to take the risk of disappointing you. If you want to accelerate your child's learning, encourage trial and error, and experimenting with alternatives.
- Avoid over-protecting your child! Children learn coping strategies and 'stickability' when things are going badly, not when they are going well.

FIGHT
Learning to tie your shoe laces

FLIGHT
Learning spellings for school

FREEZE
Reading aloud to an adult

FLOCK
Wanting to wear unsuitable clothes to school

" Every problem is also an opportunity. "

Parent pressure

Children under six benefit most from structured play, in which adults act as coaches and guides. In England and Wales, the government has introduced 'early learning goals' for three to five year olds, which outline the kind of activities that are appropriate.

Too much focus on formal learning too early can be a turn-off. Boys are particularly at risk, as they tend not to enjoy more structured work in the very early years and do better later on.

Young children also need the chance to develop social skills, as this helps them to make friends later on. Give your child opportunities to experiment on her own sometimes, as long as you're there in the background.

PAUSE FOR THOUGHT: Being honest!

Think of an occasion when you were keen to show off your child's abilities that was more about you looking good as a parent than him being a good learner. Make a note to try not to do it again!

Dealing with moods

Children have frequent mood swings. It's not surprising when you think of all the new experiences and the constant physical changes they are coping with. And moods have a major effect on learning. It's difficult to learn, for example, if you're angry or bored. Being relaxed but alert is best for learning.

Try to help your child deal with anger and calm down by distracting her: 'Let's go outside and see what Daddy is doing in the garden.' Or if she's bored, try to motivate her: 'Let's listen to the tape and learn the songs, then you'll be able to join in when we go to Jamil's school tomorrow.'

ACTIVITY: Create a mood meter with your child

1. Divide a circle of thin card into segments, as shown above.
2. Write words on it in the order shown. Make sure your child knows the meaning of all the words, or use other similar ones.
3. Make an arrow and attach it to the centre with a split pin.
4. Your child can move the arrow to show her mood. When she is feeling curious, or a word to the right of curious, she is in a good mood to learn.

The power of peer groups

Peer groups are any group your child spends time with, such as in school, church or clubs. Often, peer groups have more influence on your child than you do. If your child's friends think a fashion, pop group or computer game is 'cool', she will want to go for it.

Unfortunately, the pressure to be part of a group can stand in the way of your child's learning if the group doesn't see it as enjoyable. But you can help to influence your child's choice of peers. Do this by commenting positively about certain things: 'I like the fact that Chris always says thank you,' or 'I love Jane's enthusiasm for games; she must be fun to be with.'

Look out for unusual behaviour. Perhaps someone at school thought it was cool to be rude or anti-social, and your is child trying it out. Such testing behaviour is normal. Explain why you don't like it and suggest alternatives. Try to give her an immediate chance to practise, then praise her behaviour.

Tips for influencing your child's peer group

- Encourage your child to take up a variety of interests so that she mixes with different groups.
- Encourage her to develop a sharing attitude to toys and games.
- Hold a party for your child when it is not her birthday and use this to extend her peer group by inviting some different children.

Switching Your Child's Mind on to Learning

Children's minds are wired up to learn. However, being wired up is not the same thing as being switched on. To encourage your child to learn, help her to make connections between learning and what she'll be able to do as a result. Try saying things like: 'When you get your Proficiency badge, you can cycle to school.'

WELL DONE! YOU HAVE WON

Train Lucky properly and he might become Best in Show.

You can win at a computer game if you practise enough.

Appeal to your child's self-interest and you'll be more likely to motivate her. Computer games work like this, getting players to complete each level in order to move onto the next, more interesting one. Collecting cards works in the same way: children who don't like maths in the classroom become experts in the playground, learning the strengths or points of each card.

Collect all the stickers and you can complete your wall chart.

If you practise your cartwheels you might win the Gym Cup.

Join the Brownies and enjoy collecting all the badges.

Tips for boosting motivation

- Help your child to see the value of the big picture. Very often, when a child seems unable to settle or concentrate, it's because she doesn't fully understand what she's trying to do. Imagine doing a jigsaw without the picture on the lid and you will realise how important the big picture is.

- Help your child to set herself targets, such as learning to ride her bike without stabilizers. Talk through the process with her and make sure she knows what she has to learn or to do differently to reach each target.

- Remember that positive targets work best. Avoid using food as an incentive, and don't say things like: 'If you learn all your spellings/come top in the test/score the highest points, I'll love you forever.'

- Encourage your child to ask for help when her motivation is flagging. Two minds are better than one!

- Encourage your child to talk positively to herself: change the can'ts to cans!

Before my next birthday, I'll be able to ride my bike without stabilizers as far as the street corner.

QUICK CHECK

✓ Think about what you can do to reduce your child's anxiety.
✓ Learn how to deal with your child's moods.
✓ Don't put your child under too much pressure.
✓ Ensure your child has friends who are positive.
✓ Know how to motivate your child to learn.

Your Learning Home

Using your home for family learning

4

Have you ever wondered...

? About the best way to support your child's learning at home?

? How to organise family meals?

? What to do about TV?

? Whether your child should have a computer in their bedroom?

? What you could do outside in the garden or park?

? Which games are most helpful?

Trying some of the ideas in this chapter will help you explore these issues.

LOOKING BACK

What do you remember most about your home as a child?

Where did you do most of your learning as a child?

Where did you do most of your homework?

Did your parents read to you?

How much television did you watch?

Did you read together as a family?

LOOKING FORWARD

How would your children answer these same questions today?

How could you use each of the rooms in your home for some kind of family learning activity?

If you have a garden, how could you use it to help your child's learning?

Using Your Living Space

How you organise and use your living space can make a huge contribution to your child's learning. So why not look around you and see how to get the best out of the space you have for learning?

ACTIVITY: What happens where?

1. Create a floor plan of your house.
2. Have a family discussion about the different things you do, or could do, in different rooms.
3. Write the activities on sticky notes and stick them in the appropriate rooms. For example:
   • learning to cook in the kitchen;
   • playing the piano and using a computer in the living room;
   • learning about plants in the garden.

In the kitchen

Cookery is a great activity for learning while having fun. On days when you have more time, use a recipe and allow your child to do the measuring. Counting spoonfuls, measuring in jugs, estimating amounts, weighing, setting the oven timer and shaping dough are all valuable maths activities. Why not aim to set aside one afternoon each week or fortnight as cookery afternoon?

ACTIVITY: Go on a cupboard journey with your child

The kitchen is a great place to think about geography.

1. Choose some of the tins, fruit, pasta and other food on your shelves.
2. Study the labels and see if you can find out where they come from.
3. Either, get a map of the world and place the items on it, on their country of origin. Or, put a sticky note on each item with the country's name on it, and then line the items up with the nearest country closest to you and the most distant furthest away.
4. Discuss what you know about the countries, or go and find out more together.
   - With very young children, just focus on one country, perhaps one with which you can make some kind of connection for them.

In the dining room

Eating together is an excellent time to learn together. For many families, just getting together to eat is a challenge. Try starting with just one family meal each week, and if you usually have the TV on, make sure it is switched off on this occasion.

Tips for making eating together fun

- Let your child help to choose and cook the meal so that he is involved in the process.
- Play games while you eat (see page 93).
- Have a pile of scrap paper and pens to hand. Family restaurants have long ago realised that this helps children to be part of adult eating.

Did you know that most people are permanently dehydrated? Children need to drink at least a litre of water a day, and more if they play a lot of sport.

In the living room

Television can be a wonderful source of information and entertainment, but try to avoid having it on all the time. Working out some sensible rules for the use of television is essential if you want your family to have a good range of learning opportunities. The tips opposite will help you make the best of TV, especially with young children.

Playing the piano or keyboard is one of the most effective ways of developing a child's growing brain, so it is well worth encouraging your child to learn if possible. You will need to sit with her while she practises regularly, ideally starting with 10-15 minutes a day.

Family concerts are great for building confidence, however short and simple the piece of music played. Your child's school should be able to suggest a music teacher, or you could ring your local education authority for advice.

> **"** When my child comes home from school nowadays
> I ask him, 'What have you learned today?'
> I used to ask him, 'What have you done today?'
> but I only ever got the comment, 'Nothing.' **"**

Tips for managing TV

- With young children, watch TV with them, then talk about what you have watched. If a programme focuses on trains, get out a train set and repeat some of the words used in the programme. If it featured a particularly interesting book, borrow the book from the library, or put it on his birthday list. The more connections you make, the faster your child will learn new things.

- Talk with your child about his preferences. Then use a TV guide to plan what to watch. Tell him, for example, 'Your favourite programme is on television at one o'clock. We'll be out then, but I'll record it for us to watch when we get home.' Try to keep a selection of good videotapes to use when you need to occupy him while you do an important task or make a phone call.

- Establish some simple rules about the amount of TV you watch. You could make two evenings a week 'no TV nights', when you play a family game or do something else together. As your child gets older, discuss any concerns you have about TV and try to reach a compromise.

In the bedroom

Your child's bedroom has a special importance for him. Even if it is shared with other children, it is the closest thing to his own space.

Bedtime patterns are especially important in establishing good learning behaviour. Always try to read your child a story. Until he is able to read on his own, hear him read a few paragraphs to you first, then read a book to him. As soon as he can read on his own, you read to him first and then leave him to read to himself.

Some children like to listen to a story tape to get off to sleep, so allow time for this. For example, if you want your child to go to sleep at 8.30pm, aim to have him in bed and be reading to him at least 45 minutes before this.

Bookshelves.
Books could be sorted by type of book, date first read, or favourites.

T.V. or computer.
If you allow these in your child's room, agree family rules about their use.

Beanbag.
Make sure your child has a cosy place to read with good natural light.

In the bathroom

The bath makes an excellent science laboratory. Try your own experiments with water or buy kits from toy shops. Bathtime is also a great opportunity to chat. Your child is 'captive' in the bath and you can ask questions that he may be too busy to hear properly during the rest of the day.

Encourage your child to find out what floats and what sinks.

Make a waterwheel from a cork and four pieces of cardboard.

Tips for creating a learning environment

- Make sure your child's play area has good natural light and is not too hot. When you are too hot you do not learn as well.
- Store toys and books in a logical way, labelling boxes and cupboards. Draw your child's attention to the ways in which the toys and books are gathered, sorted and tidied.
- Be aware of how people react to different colours. For example, red is linked with creative thinking and high energy, blue is for study and concentration. If in doubt, use light colours!
- Create a special place to put photographs of your child with certificates or other positive messages.
- Remember that the internet is also a great learning environment (see page 96). Ⓦ

In the garden

If you have a garden, you have an outdoor classroom which is great for developing maths skills and finding out about science. If not, many activities can be done in a local park.

A wigwam is easy to make from bamboo poles and an old sheet.

Buddleia attracts butterflies.

Let your child have her own bit of garden for growing things.

Nasturtiums are fast growing so are great for young gardeners.

Try growing favourite vegetables.

PAUSE FOR THOUGHT: Maths in the garden or park

When your child plays on climbing frames, compare how tall he is against you. Try to find opportunities to talk about wide or narrow shapes. Use words such as forwards, backwards, on top, underneath, in front of, behind, above and below. Always encourage him to tell you what he is doing.

When playing ball games, ask him to fetch the longest bat or the smallest ball. Measure out the area for a game in paces, and talk about different shapes and sizes of equipment.

QUICK CHECK

✓ Use every room in your home to help your family learning.
✓ It's worth making the effort to have family meals.
✓ Have some rules for the use of TV and computers.
✓ Play some of the games you played when you were a child.

Classrooms on Your Doorstep

Getting the best out of your local area

5

Have you ever wondered...

? What your local library has to offer and how to get the most out of it?

? What your local museum has to offer?

? Where to go for interesting and educational trips?

? About getting your child into clubs?

? What you could do to make family car journeys easier?

? What to do with your child in school holidays?

Trying some of the ideas in this chapter will help you explore these issues.

There are lots of great places to visit on your doorstep, wherever you live. Try some of the ideas in this chapter. Some of them work well on family journeys, too.

? Did you know that more people visit museums every year than attend football matches?

PLACES TO LEARN

DO YOU KNOW WHERE TO FIND YOUR NEAREST...

	Yes	No		Yes	No
Library?			Theatre?		
Museum?			Cinema?		
Historic house?			Leisure centre?		
Farm or animal sanctuary?			College?		
Woodland or park?			Football or athletics club?		
Gallery?			Internet café?		

WHEN WAS THE LAST TIME YOU VISITED A...

	IN THE LAST 6 MONTHS	MORE THAN 6 MONTHS AGO		IN THE LAST 6 MONTHS	MORE THAN 6 MONTHS AGO
Library?			Theatre?		
Museum?			Cinema?		
Historic house?			Leisure centre?		
Farm / animal sanctuary?			College?		
Woodland or park?			Football or athletics club?		
Gallery?			Internet café?		

DO YOU KNOW WHERE TO GO TO...

	Yes	No		Yes	No
Find out more about wildlife?			Learn how to paint?		
Join a theatre group?			Watch birds?		
Join a football / cricket team?			Learn how to cook?		
Go for an interesting walk?			Go fishing?		
Dance or have dance lessons?			Learn computer skills?		

" Small keys open big doors. "

Finding Out What's Available

Most learning is informal – it results from an interest. For example, planning a holiday abroad, you might go to the library for guide books; or, intrigued by posters for an exhibition in a local art gallery, you might take your family and find that the gallery is running free taster activities. As long as you know what's available, you can decide whether you're interested! Ⓦ

Every year, on the second weekend in October, the UK *Campaign for Learning* runs Family Learning Weekend Ⓦ to raise awareness of what libraries, museums, colleges, parks, sport centres, cinemas, shopping centres and many other places have to offer. Hundreds of thousands of families get involved, many for the first time, in thousands of events nationwide.

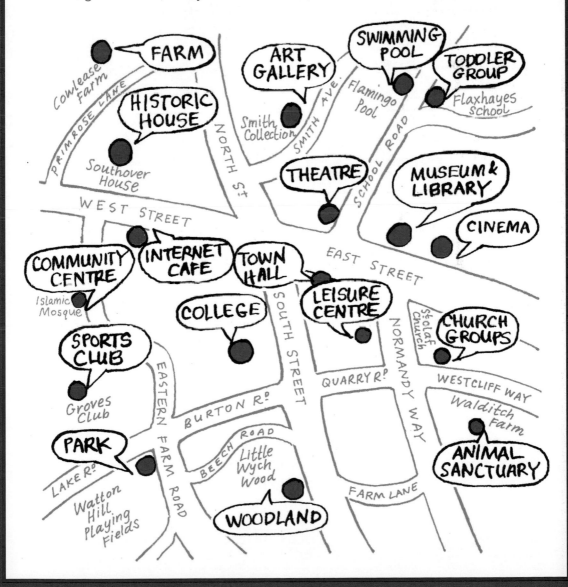

Learning about libraries

Nowadays, most libraries are like friendly learning centres. Whatever you want to know about – internet access, photocopying, children's story tapes or videos, music CDs and tapes, how to find specific books – the librarians will be delighted to help. They'll also tell you about book clubs and activities.

Many libraries run activities for children.

Many have extra school holiday activities.

Authors read their stories.

Book clubs such as DADS AND LADS are popular.

Joining your local library is easy: pick up information to take home to read, or join on the spot. Most libraries need to see a household bill or something similar as proof of your name and address, and proof of your signature, such as a driving licence.

Tips for getting the best out of your library

- Establish a routine for library visits, perhaps after school once a week, or every Saturday morning. Take time to browse with your child, helping her to choose books. If appropriate, make sure both parents are involved.
- Remember that libraries have much more than books to offer.
- Show your enthusiasm for books by choosing some for yourself, too.

Making the most of museums

Museums are treasure troves! Few people in Britain live more than an hour away from one. There are museums for science, furniture, technology, inventions, tanks, ships, nursing, rural life, design, clothes, jewellery, prison life, children, plants, natural history, environmental education, toys and much more. In addition, historic houses, such as those owned by the National Trust, are a kind of living museum.

Tips for getting the best out of museums

- Plan a trip to a city where there are several museums to choose from.
- If you have a local museum, ask if they take part in Family Learning Weekend or if they run an educational programme.
- As a family, make a list of things you are interested in and then look for a museum that fits with these. The internet can be very useful for this.

ACTIVITY: Make a museum of chairs

1. With your child, look at the chairs in your home. You'll be surprised at the variety, which may include one from a grandparent or other older relative.
2. Ask relatives to tell you anything they can about older chairs, especially if you have one from Victorian times or earlier. How are the chairs different?
3. Get a book on furniture from the library, and find out anything else you can about your chairs. Make some notes about them.
4. Plan a weekend to invite family and friends to visit your museum. Set the chairs out in order of how old you think they are. Suggest to your child that he might be the guide. You will all learn lots of history in the process.

Joining clubs

There are clubs for just about everything from music, drama and art to sporting interests. Remember the established favourites, cubs and brownies, too. Find out about clubs in the What's On section in your local paper, at the library, at your local community centre, on supermarket notice boards, or in school, playgroup, church or other faith group. Talking to other parents and listening to local radio will give you ideas, too.

ACROBATICS

WATER FUN

MAKING GIANTS

NATURE WALKS

Did you know that about half of a person's learning ability develops by the age of four and 80% by the age of eight?

By joining a club, your child will extend her friendship group. She will also begin to develop the habit of learning and find out about commitment, as well as explore her interests in a secure environment.

Holiday Time

School holidays and travel are wonderful opportunities for learning new things. Here are some ideas for making holidays fun for all the family.

Tips for getting ready for journeys

- Have a family brainstorm of things you could do in a car, train, or plane.
- Get children to make up travel bags with favourite games and toys.
- Take lots of story tapes. Give children personal stereos and headphones if you want some periods of peace and quiet.

Car journey games

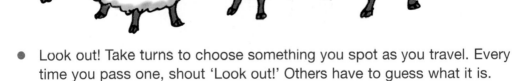

- Look out! Take turns to choose something you spot as you travel. Every time you pass one, shout 'Look out!' Others have to guess what it is.
- Buy Eye-spy books or play *I spy with my little eye*, which is a great game for all ages. For very young children, spy things 'the colour of...' rather than 'beginning with the letter...'
- Take turns to choose a car number plate and make one or more words from the letters. Score a point for every letter you use. Give younger children an 'e' or an 'a' that they can use whenever they want.
- Spot car makes. Score points on a scale of 1-5, giving most points for the less common makes. For example, 5 for a Porsche, 1 for a Ford Fiesta.
- Tell a story. Take turns to build up a story, sentence by sentence.
- Spot the number. First to spot numbers 1 to 20 on number plates wins.
- Take turns to be a DJ and introduce a favourite track from a CD or tape.

Fun at home

● Make a family flag. Use an old, preferably plain, pillowcase and draw lines on one side to divide it into four panels. In each panel, paint or sew pictures that show what you like doing and what is important to you as a family. You might like to make up a family motto to go along the bottom.

● Create a photo collage for the kitchen wall. Stick your favourite holiday photos onto a large piece of paper. Think about what anyone in them might have been saying and add speech bubbles with felt-tip pens. You might also like to add drawings and diary notes of your memories.

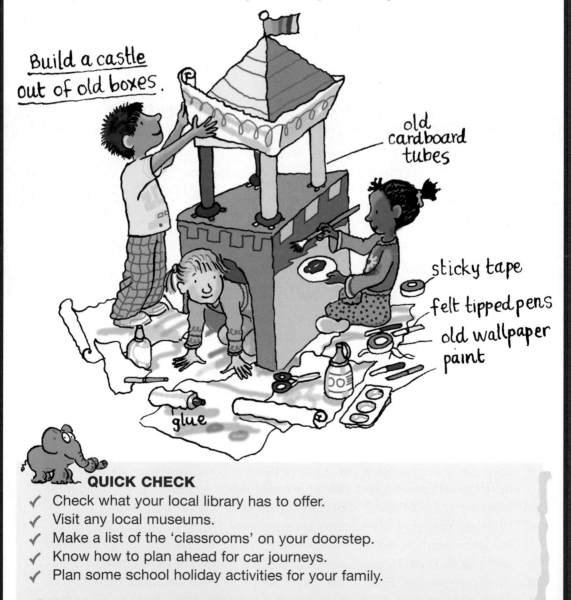

Build a castle out of old boxes.

old cardboard tubes

sticky tape

felt tipped pens

old wallpaper paint

glue

QUICK CHECK
✓ Check what your local library has to offer.
✓ Visit any local museums.
✓ Make a list of the 'classrooms' on your doorstep.
✓ Know how to plan ahead for car journeys.
✓ Plan some school holiday activities for your family.

Getting Unstuck
Learning the benefits of being positive

6

Have you ever wondered...

? How to be more positive?

? What to do when you get stuck?

? Why you don't like taking risks?

? Why your child sometimes gives up so easily?

? How to be more creative?

? How to manage anger?

Trying some of the ideas in this chapter will help you explore these issues.

Chapter 1 introduced the benefits of being positive. This chapter gives more practical ideas and introduces you to the '3 Ps' of positive parenting: positivity, persistence and problem-solving.

? Did you know that if you know where you're going and set goals, you're more likely to succeed?

HOW POSITIVE IS YOUR PARENTING?

ALWAYS   NEVER
+2 Marks   -1 Mark

1. You're about to go out for the evening when your baby is sick over your new clothes. You smile and say, 'We'll laugh about this in years to come!' ....

2. Your child has a favourite bedtime book. He asks you to read it again and again. You do so...

3. Your child doesn't believe your explanation of why birds don't fall off branches. You try a more creative approach.................

4. Going to the bathroom in the middle of the night, you slip on some lego bricks and crack your head on a dumper truck. Your first thought is how to improve the toy storage.........................

5. Your child joins a swimming club. You agree to take her there every weekday at 6.00am and to competitions all day Saturday........

6. Your child gets upset as he struggles with a jigsaw. You avoid interfering because you want him to learn to do it for himself..........

7. Your child comes last in a school sports race. You spend the evening persuading her that she is brilliant at football......................

8. You want to go home to watch a major event on TV. Your child wants you to carry on pushing him on the swings in the park. You willingly agree and forgo your own pleasure.............................

9. You're relaxing on a Sunday evening. Your son and his friends are enjoying a karaoke session, when the machine's batteries run out. You all pool your ideas as to which shops might still be open....

Score 2 marks for each Always and take off 1 mark for each Never.

Questions 1, 4, 7 are 'Positivity' questions.
Questions 2, 5, 8 are 'Persistence' questions.
Questions 3, 6, 9 are 'Problem-solving' questions.

Score 9 -18 You are a superstar – a model of positivity!
Score 0 - 9   Some work is needed – this chapter will help!
Less than 0   Go and lie down in a darkened room!

The First P: Being Positive

What you say to your child has a huge impact on him. To be a good learner, your child needs to have positive views about learning and about his chances of success in learning. These views come from you! As chapter 1 showed, your child's attitudes and assumptions mirror your own.

Three ways to help your child be positive

1 Listen to what you say

Take time at the end of the day to reflect on how you talked to your child. Think about whether you have given out positive or negative messages. Negative messages might include: putting your child down, unfavourable comparisons, expressing annoyance at his behaviour, or threats. Positive messages and describing what you want – rather than what you don't want – are most likely to help you get what you want.

2 Catch your child being successful

When your child does something well, or improves on a previous effort, notice it and praise it. If it's something he can repeat, ask him to show you again. Catch and celebrate success of all sorts, not just academic success.

3 See life through the positive window

Help your child take a positive approach every time! When he says, 'I'm no good at...' remind him how much better he has become and how much better he can be. Help him to replace 'I got a low score' with 'I'll get a better score next time', or 'I can't do this' with 'What will it be like when I can?'

Tip for giving your child a positive 'message'

- If your child is anxious about something, give him a positive 'message' that he can 'pull out of his pocket'. For example, if he's worried about a test at school, give him the 'message' that you will stop whatever you're doing to think about him at the time the test starts. He will know that while he's doing the test, you're supporting him. Do not actually give him a written message as this may get him into trouble!

The Second P: Being Persistent

Persistence is the ability to stick at something. When faced with difficulty or uncertainty, many of us retreat back into our 'comfort zone' – familiar territory where we feel safe. If we grow up feeling we need the safe alternative, we stop taking risks. And learning is a risk. Real learning takes place when we are at the edge of our comfort zone.

If your child knows from experience that he can cope with difficulties, he'll look for challenges and overcome new problems. But if you make things too easy for him, he won't learn to persist. Children with low persistence give up too easily and do less well in life.

> Unless you do something beyond what you can already do, you will never grow and develop.

Three ways to help your child develop persistence

1 Focus on what you want your child to achieve

For your child to succeed at something, he needs to have the end in mind. For example, knowing what a house might look like will help him build one from plastic bricks. It's also important to talk to him about what it will feel like when he can do something. If he has thought about what it will feel like to do a forward roll, he's more likely to keep going until he has done one.

2 Practise practising

Practice involves checking, adjusting, experimenting and moving on. We learn when we see something isn't right, then make an adjustment and do it better, rather than when we simply repeat the same thing. Practising can be frustrating. But it's vital that your child experiences frustration so he learns to work through it. When you practise reading together, for example, encourage him to experiment with new words. Gradually, he'll do this for himself and not get frustrated when he can't immediately read a word.

We deal with frustration in different ways. How does your child try to cope? Does he persist or give up? If he persists, does he...

...talk himself through it?

...slow down and try step-by-step?

...stop and start again?

...stand back and think of another way?

...go off and do something else, then come back to it?

If he comes to you for help, or needs you to encourage or cajole him, he's not developing his own coping strategies. Stand back! It's better for him to practise and develop ways of coping now.

3 Explore alternative solutions

Giving up is easy. We are encouraged to give up by the belief that there is only one answer or one correct way to do something. Too many school tests reinforce the idea that there is only one answer.

Encourage your child to think about alternatives. Try it in your daily life! With a pre-school child, take different routes to the shops, experiment with different furniture layouts in their bedroom, or try different breakfast cereals.

Did you know that it takes about 3,500 hours of practice for a young instrumentalist to become a good musician?

The Third P: Problem-solving

Problem-solving is an essential life skill. To help your child become a problem-solver, encourage curiosity. Asking lots of questions is as useful in learning as finding answers.

Encourage your child to seek explanations and discover things for himself. Don't always give him neat answers to questions. Enjoy exploring open-ended questions, which have no simple answers, with him.

The posters below were created by children working with the *Campaign for Learning* to encourage their friends to be curious and come up with good ideas.

Three ways to help your child become a problem-solver

1 Tune to his curiosity channel

Young children are naturally curious! Here's an example of four children showing their curiosity in learning about how babies are made.

> Babies come when you're not looking. My mummy went away and when she came back she had a baby.

> You need lots of water and blood and bones and things. You have to save up the tears so that the baby can have a drink.

> Where does the water come from? It must come from somewhere, maybe there's a place where you can get blood and bones and stuff.

> My dad says that parents make their own babies. He must be right 'cos my mum says she was asleep and ask your dad.

ACTIVITY: Use problem-solving games

1. Think of some problems in your home or neighbourhood, such as: How can we do less housework? How can we use less electricit? How could we stop graffiti in the street?

2. Use these two games to come up with as many solutions as possible:
   - 'Put on heads': think of how someone you know might approach the problem and imagine you're 'wearing' their head. You may reach some different solutions.
   - 'Borrowed genius': think about what someone who was really brilliant at something would have done to solve the problem. Get your child to pretend he is that person and tackle the problem in stages.

2 Think up good questions

A key learning skill is being able to ask good questions – ones that may have several answers. Children learn from questions and not just from answers.

Use these key words to help your child think up good questions:

3 Make connections

Learning occurs when we make connections between something new and things we already know or have experienced. Encourage your child to make comparisons. Ask, 'What's this like?', 'When did we see it before?', 'What does this remind you of?'.

Mind maps™ are a great way of organising information so that you can see connections between things. Children can begin to create simple mind maps™ like the one opposite from about five years old.

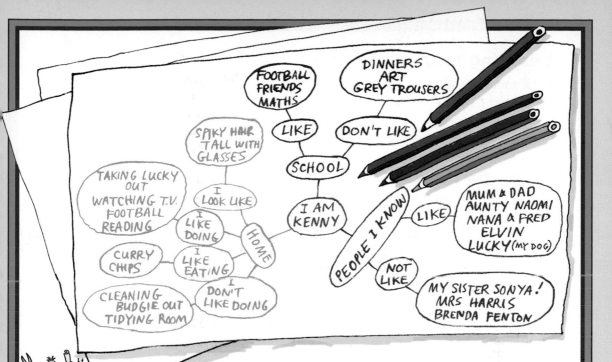

ACTIVITY: Make an 'All About Me' mind map™

1. You will need paper and coloured pencils.
2. Help your child choose a few words to describe himself and write these down.
3. Make lists of: things he likes doing at home; things he dislikes doing at home; things he likes doing at school; things he dislikes doing at school; people he knows, including family members and relatives; favourite things such as foods, TV programmes or clothes.
4. Sort the words under four headings: home, school, people and me.
5. Write your child's name in the centre of a large sheet of paper in one colour.
6. Draw three short lines from his name in different colours, and write 'home', 'school' and 'people' in circles at the end of these.
7. Draw lines branching out from these for the words in each of his lists.

While you are creating the mind map™, talk through what you are doing and why. Point out the connections and patterns. Encourage your child to predict what should go where.

Did you know that when asked what he would do if he had an hour to live, Einstein replied that he would spend 55 minutes searching for the right question – finding the answer would only take 5 minutes?

65

Learning to Control Anger

Children may get angry because they feel they are constantly failing or getting stuck, or can't solve a problem while others have the answer.

Here's a way to teach your child how to control his temper. Point out the pause button on a video recorder which stops a video immediately. Help him develop the ability to press this button when required, using the tips below.

Tips for controlling anger

- Count to 10 or have a secret phrase that you repeat in your head whenever you're about to lose your temper.
- Use 'traffic lights': when someone does or says something that is annoying, imagine the light is on red, and wait. Visualize it changing to orange, and get ready to walk away. When it turns green, walk away.
- Imagine that the person making you angry is a giant green frog. Imagine them looking like a frog, sounding like a frog, hopping about like a frog, but say nothing! Having a laugh helps to make anger go away.

QUICK CHECK

✓ Remember to catch your child being successful.
✓ Try to be more positive.
✓ Practise!
✓ Get your child to explore alternative solutions.
✓ Encourage curiosity.
✓ Help your child make connections.
✓ Teach your child to control anger.

7

You've Got a Friend

Exploring how friends and family can help

Have you ever wondered...

? How to involve members of your family in helping your child?

? Why your child sometimes prefers to talk to your parents?

? Whether you could choose some of your child's friends?

Trying some of the ideas in this chapter will help you explore these issues.

This chapter looks at the many ways in which members of your wider family and friends can offer support and help your child to learn.

? Did you know that the world our children live in is changing four times faster than our schools are?

WHAT DO YOU THINK?

A recent poll conducted in the UK among 11-15 year olds showed that:

84% respect their parents more than anyone else; more than half respect teachers, police officers and doctors.

84% think it is important that parents stay together while their children grow up.

Children living with single or step-parents average **5 minutes** more homework a night than children living with both parents.

94% say there is some bullying in their school; **63%** have been bullied at school.

One in three has played truant on at least one occasion, but only **3%** have done so regularly.

The average time spent watching television is **11 hours 45 minutes** a week – six times longer than is spent reading.

Only **one in five** play a musical instrument.

41% spend no time on computer games, and of the remainder that use them, **14%** do so for only an hour a week.

41% never pick up a book out of school and the highest number that do, **23%**, only read for an hour each week.

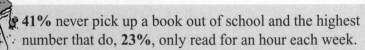

Talk about how true these statements are for you and your family now.

Involving Other Family Members and Friends

The children's card game Happy Families was created around a 'typical' family of two parents and two children. But things have changed and children now grow up in many different kinds of family groups.

Many children live mainly in one parent families.

Many children have step-parents.

Friends may be treated as family, sharing meals and helping with children.

Too many parents exhaust themselves, thinking they have to be responsible for helping their child do everything. But, whatever your family arrangements, there are always other adults who might help. It's tough but essential that you check out all the people who spend time with your child.

- Grandparents are a special case – see page 72 for some ideas about how they might help your child learn.
- Uncles, aunts and cousins might share their hobbies with your child, take her on day trips or provide safe homes in which she can experience her first sleepovers.
- Step-parents can often help with reading, homework and everything else covered in this book, simply because they don't have a biological relationship and so can provide a fresh approach.
- In the Christian tradition children have godparents, who are often close friends of the parents and who take a special interest in the child. Many families with other beliefs have versions of this special relationship.

Why not use the activity on page 70 to think about members of your wider family, and how they might be able to help you and your child?

> **No one family is the same. But every family has its everyday geniuses if it can only make time to find them.**

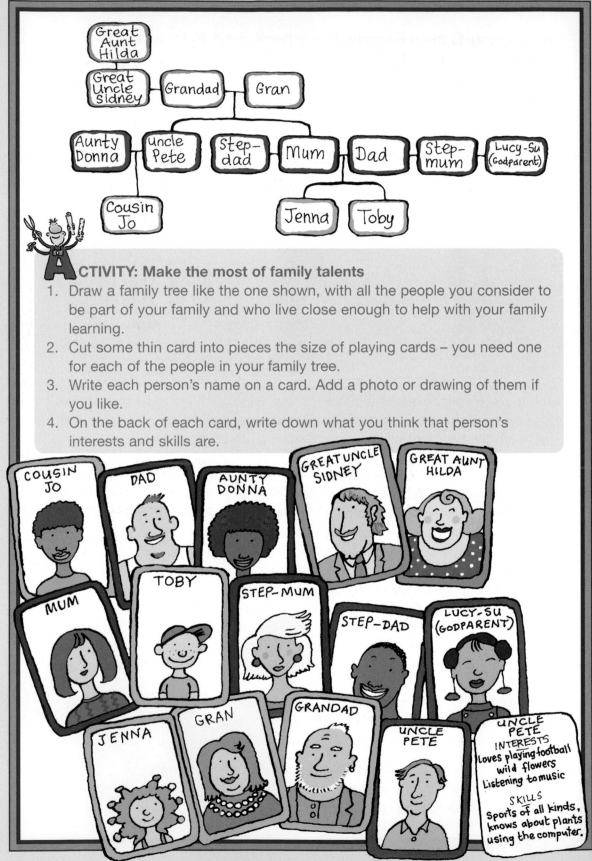

ACTIVITY: Make the most of family talents

1. Draw a family tree like the one shown, with all the people you consider to be part of your family and who live close enough to help with your family learning.
2. Cut some thin card into pieces the size of playing cards – you need one for each of the people in your family tree.
3. Write each person's name on a card. Add a photo or drawing of them if you like.
4. On the back of each card, write down what you think that person's interests and skills are.

Grandparents are wonderful!

Grandparents are among the most special of the adults who can help your child learn. They have an enormous wealth of experience, which they are normally delighted to share with their grandchildren. If you're lucky, one or more will live close enough for your child to see them regularly. Why not suggest some of the ideas on page 72 to them?

Your child may find it easier to talk about some things with her grandparents than she does with you. This is quite normal. Give her space to do so. It will be good for her to hear another perspective from someone who has her best interests at heart. Grandparents may have time to coach your child with reading, maths or anything else she needs a little extra one-on-one time for.

Like other close family members, grandparents can provide a safe place for your child's first nights away from home. A sleepover with grandparents allows her to see the world from another generation's viewpoint.

Activities for grandparents to share with children

- Get out an old photograph album and talk about family members. If possible, share funny stories about them. This helps children remember who the people are. Talk about what life was like for you when you were a child.

- Dig out games you may have from your own childhood. Children love to play different games with different people. Even though they may be only interested in hi-tech gadgets at home, playing Happy Families or Snap with a grandparent is fun.

- Interviewing grandparents and recording their memories is great fun for a child, especially finding out what it was like at school when they were young. This activity can produce a wonderful living history lesson.

- If possible, visit the area where you grew up as a child. Children love to make connections like this and it creates a living geography lesson for them.

- Suggest your child invites a grandparent to get involved in something to do with her school. They might do the school run one day to get a better idea of what her school is like, or have a look at some of her school books.

Being with her grandparents gives your child the opportunity of learning to care for others. She can fetch and carry, help and support. But while she has a lot to learn, she can also teach. Many grandparents are less confident with computers than their children or grandchildren. It's great for a child to teach her grandparent how to use e-mail or the internet!

The most precious thing any child can give a grandparent is time. The activity on page 73 is something that does this. Show it to your child – she might like to try it!

YEAR 4

ACTIVITY: Make a present of time

Here's an idea for your child to make a special present for a grandparent.

1. Design a set of vouchers like the one below, on a computer if possible, each one of which is a 'gift of time'. For example, one voucher might be for helping Nana with jobs around her house and another for showing her how to send an e-mail.
2. Make a wallet to put the vouchers in.
3. Give the wallet as a birthday or other special present.

PAY *Nana*
2 hours help
around the house.
(valid until Sept.)
Lila khan

SUNSHINE BANK

LILA KHAN

The benefits of having a mentor

Chapter 3 suggested ideas for helping to 'choose' or influence your child's friends. One of the most important influences for a child is older friends. Schools have picked up on this and started to introduce mentors – young people who give some of their time to guiding and supporting those younger than themselves. In primary schools, 9 and 10 year olds have been paired up with 15 year olds from secondary schools.

This can be an excellent experience for both mentors and those being mentored. Mentors enjoy the feeling of being asked for their advice, and those being mentored benefit from sharing ideas and concerns with someone older, who is not an adult.

Why not put this into practice for your child?

If there is a mature teenager in your family network who would be able to take on a mentoring role, speak directly to her or him. Ask whether they would be interested in becoming an informal mentor and spending time occasionally with your child. Let them know how grateful you would be and take the opportunity to say how much you admire the way they are going about things.

74

8

Words and Sums

Helping your child with literacy and numeracy

Have you ever wondered...

? How to choose a good book for your child?

? How to help your child with learning to read?

? How writing is taught in school nowadays?

? How to help your child with spelling?

? What kind of maths children are taught now?

? What you can do to help before your child goes to school?

Trying some of the ideas in this chapter will help you explore these issues.

Many of us feel uncertain when it comes to helping our children with reading, writing and maths. This chapter aims to give you more confidence and help you to understand how children learn to use words and numbers.

Did you know that Shakespeare spelled his own name in a number of different ways?

HOW CONFIDENT ARE YOU ABOUT YOUR OWN SKILLS?

	Yourself Yes	No	Your partner Yes	No
1. Do you find it difficult to make time to read?.....................	☐	☐	☐	☐
2. Are you worried that you don't have the right books in your home?..	☐	☐	☐	☐
3. Do you worry when you don't know what a word means?...	☐	☐	☐	☐
4. Are you embarrassed when you spell words wrongly?........	☐	☐	☐	☐
5. Do you find maths hard?...	☐	☐	☐	☐
6. Did you find learning English and maths hard when you were young?.......................................	☐	☐	☐	☐
7. Do you worry that the way your child is taught English (literacy) and maths (numeracy) at school is different from how you were taught it?..............................	☐	☐	☐	☐

Take heart if you've answered 'yes' to any of these questions – you're normal! There's no such thing, for example, as having the 'right' books at home: 'reading friendly' homes have fiction, non-fiction, recipe books, DIY guides and so on, as well as magazines and newspapers.

PAUSE FOR THOUGHT: Reading matters!

Have you ever thought of reading together as a family? Why not make one night a week reading night, sharing a chapter or two each time? You could discuss your reading at family mealtimes. It's also good to encourage your child to lend books to friends and borrow some in return.

Learning to Read

Before your child goes to school

As soon as your child can sit in your lap, share books and stories with him. Go for books with covers that you like the look of – he will pick up on your enthusiasm. Pop-up books, waterproof bath books, board books, fabric books and books with sound-effects are all great. If family or friends ask what to get him for a present say, 'Books!'

Try and make regular times to read every day. If your routine includes a bedtime story, have other times when your child is less tired and you can spend time looking at the pictures and print. You'll find 5-15 minutes is about right for most young children. Aim to read two books at each session: one chosen by your child and one by you. This way, you can read a variety of books, while your child develops personal preferences.

If you have a new baby, try sharing a book with your child while you're giving your baby her feed. This has the extra benefit of focusing attention on your child at a time when he might be experiencing jealousy. Encourage him to get a favourite cuddly toy and snuggle up beside you as you all settle down in a comfortable chair.

Did you know that infants use their long term memory to store spoken words before they can speak them? Word learning may begin as early as around 8 months.

Tips for choosing books for young children

- The golden rule is – select books that look fun!
- Books that have repeating phrases or rhymes make it easier for your child to join in as you read.
- Choose a variety of stories, factual books, activity books, nursery rhyme and poetry books.

At some stage, your child will start to 'play' at reading, just as he 'plays' at being a postman or a nurse. Try the following to help him develop his skills.

- Encourage him to point to the text when he 'reads'.
- Let him 'read' to you.
- Allow him to make up the story; he is experimenting with language and modelling his behaviour on yours.
- Talk of 'letters', 'words' and 'sentences'.
- Point out full stops, exclamation marks, speech marks and capital letters.
- Show him that sentences and names always begin with a capital letter. He won't understand this fully yet, but it will speed his learning in due course.

Did you know that seven year olds given books at nine months have achieved results 20% higher than other children in national tests?

PAUSE FOR THOUGHT: Fun and games with language

Action rhymes are great for young children – actions help them to remember words, and rhythm, rhyme and repetition all encourage joining in. Why not look out for music and rhyme sessions in your neighbourhood? Many games help develop reading skills, too (see page 93).

Tips for encouraging reading

For toddlers

- Read with your child every day.
- Take time to look at and talk about the pictures.
- Encourage your child to turn the pages.
- Encourage him to join in with repeating phrases.
- Use your finger to follow the print occasionally.
- Make sure he sees you reading for pleasure.

For pre-school children

- Read a variety, including poems, comics, magazines.
- Get your child to look at pictures and predict what will happen in a story.
- Make sure your child sees you reading (recipes, newspapers, food packaging instructions etc.) and writing (shopping lists, messages etc.). Remember to read aloud when he is around!
- Look at street names, shop signs, road signs and car number plates.

For school-age children

- Read to your child, then let him read to you.
- Allow time for self-correction if he makes a mistake.
- Encourage him to talk about what he has read, and to retell stories.
- Buy him games with instructions to read and follow.
- Make birthday cards, invitations, lists and messages together and encourage him to write letters and postcards.

Learning to Write

Before your child goes to school

Give your child paper and pencils that are big enough for him to grip easily and make a satisfying mark on paper. Join him in using chalks and a blackboard, wax crayons, felt-tip pens (with washable ink) and colouring pencils. Finger paints are great if you have space for messy activities.

Use bath time for drawing and 'writing' with crayons that can be used on the bath.

Writing involves three skills:

- Handwriting: learning to write letters and join them up;
- Creative thinking: enthusiasm for writing about something;
- Grammar: the organisation of thoughts into words, sentences and paragraphs that make sense.

Help your child start learning to write letters by practising her name. You might show her how to write mummy, daddy, and any brothers' or sisters' names, too. Better still, encourage her 'free' writing. When you write a note for Grandma or a shopping list, get her to do the same. Her early writing will be scribble, but just as her baby sounds mimicked you speaking before she could talk, so her scribbles will represent symbols, letters and eventually words. Why not turn a playhouse or a corner of your kitchen or living room into a pretend office or shop?

Toddlers often produce pages of squiggles that they want to 'read' aloud. Listen to your child's story carefully and talk to him about it. Encourage him to use any letters he knows, such as 'm' for mummy. Children use the correct letter at the beginning of words before they use the correct final letter. They take longer again to learn the middle vowel sounds.

Encouraging school-age children

> ### Writing Rules for older children
> 1. Have I stopped mixing up capital and lower case letters?
> 2. Am I careful with my spellings?
> 3. Are my tall letters tall and do my tails go below the line?
> 4. Do I write clearly and joined up and with spaces between the words?
> 5. Do I write in sentences using full stops and capital letters?
> 6. Do I revise my work to improve it?
> 7. Can I edit my work to correct it?
> 8. Do I use adventurous words?
> 9. Do I describe things and write about feelings?
> 10. Can I use conjunctions such as but, when, after, so, because?
> 11. Have I got commas in some sentences?
> 12. Do I use speech marks and other punctuation properly?
> 13. Do I use paragraphs?
> 14. Will the person reading this understand and enjoy it?

Tips for helping your child with spelling

- Encourage your child to have a go. Praise him for a word spelled correctly.
- Don't over-correct your child's spelling.
- Be aware that he may write words as they sound, such as 'telfon' for telephone. Gradually point out how such words are actually spelled.
- Try to find four correct spellings for each one that you point out is wrong.
- Help him to check his own spellings. The simplest method is: look, cover, write, say, check. He looks at a word, then covers it up, writes down how he thinks it is spelled, reads this aloud, and finally checks for accuracy.
- Play word games (see page 93). Try the number plate game on car journeys (see page 53).
- Encourage your child to use a dictionary, or a spellchecker on a computer.

PAUSE FOR THOUGHT: Learning to spell

Did spelling come easily to you? If so, try to remember what you found most difficult and how you overcame it. If not, make a list of anything that helped. Have these thoughts in the back of your mind as you try to help your child.

Tips for encouraging writing

For toddlers

- Write to, with and around your child.
- Draw letters and numbers with your finger in the air, on a table, or in a sandpit.
- Trace letter shapes in alphabet books, holding your hand over his.
- Have lots of paper, felt-tips and pencils for play.
- Put up alphabet and number posters in your child's bedroom.
- Use magnetic letters, plastic letter tiles and stencils.

For pre-school children

- Encourage him to talk himself through his 'writing' while he does it, and to read it back to you.
- Encourage him to 'write' from left to right and top to bottom, and to leave spaces between 'words'.
- If possible, give him a place to write by a pinboard or wall, where you can display his writing and drawings.
- Make an alphabet book with a page for each letter.
- Together, write the words for everyday things on their correct pages. Find pictures to cut out of magazines for each word and add to the page.
- Have a 'letter of the day'. Stick it up somewhere prominent, then find words that begin with that letter.

For school-age children

- Make sure your child sees you writing, so he thinks of it as an adult activity.
- Praise your child's writing and only comment on neatness or accuracy afterwards. Be specific: 'You've described that spider really well. I can almost feel it crawling up my leg.'
- Give your child a junior dictionary. Make sure he knows how to use it.
- Encourage writing for different purposes. Point out differences in the way we use language, depending on who we are writing to.

Learning about Maths

Before your child goes to school

Nobody is 'no good' at maths. Some people find maths easy, and some find it harder. Believe it or not, we do maths all the time – when you measure wood for a shelf, weigh ingredients for a cake, or check your watch to work out how long you've got for doing something. Such everyday activities can make maths fun and accelerate your child's mathematical understanding. Chapter 4 includes ideas for maths in the kitchen and garden or park.

Tips for encouraging counting

- When you lay the table – count the plates, cups, knives, forks and spoons.
- Count when you walk up or down steps.
- Count the coins when giving older brothers or sisters their bus fare.
- Count spoons of sugar into cups of tea.
- Count as you tidy away clean socks.
- Count the items out of the bags after a shopping trip.

Aaron – Do you think I have enough balls of wool to finish this jumper?

As your child begins to understand the 'two-ness of two' or the 'three-ness of three', encourage him to estimate numbers.

Make activities relevant and fun. If your child thinks he is helping you by counting the socks, or the screws in a jar, he is learning that maths is important for everyday living.

PAUSE FOR THOUGHT: Fun and games with maths

Music, rhythm and rhyme all help children learn number skills. Get CDs, cassettes, videos or books of number songs and nursery rhymes to sing and chant together. Playing card games, dominoes and board games with counters and dice help develop skills, too. Your child won't even think about the fact that he's doing maths! Why not have a weekly 'Games Night', where the whole family enjoy board games together?

The four rules of number

Adding, subtracting, dividing and multiplying are often called 'the four rules of number'. Here's how you can introduce them to your child in everyday activities.

Adding and subtracting

When preparing a meal, for example, you might say: 'We've put out two yoghurts and two bananas. Can you add up how many things that is altogether? Have we got enough for everybody to have something?' Using the correct words will help him learn that to 'add up' means to give the total. Ask him to 'take away' or 'subtract' if there are too many items. Encourage him to say what he is doing, such as, 'We've got two yoghurts and three bananas. That makes five altogether. But there are only four of us – Janine, Sam, Mummy, and me. I'll take away one banana, then that makes four!'

Dividing

Talking about division is easy when you cut up a pie or cake, share out the segments of an orange or deal out playing cards, for example. Whenever possible, encourage your child's involvement. A pack of sweets is great for division! Give him three bowls and suggest he divides the sweets so that there are the same number in each bowl. He can either share with two friends or you can keep back two of the bowls for later.

Let's cut this apple in half – that's two pieces – and we'll have half each.

Multiplying

Packing a family picnic, you might decide to take two drinks for each person, so you need to multiply the number of people by two. Ask your child to count out the drinks: 'Can you put out two drinks for each of us – that's two for you, two for me, and two for Jamie? That's three lots of two, or three times two. How many drinks do we need altogether? Let's count together!'

Shape, size, measurement and pattern

Maths is not just about numbers! Understanding and using shape, size, measurement and pattern are also essential maths skills. Art and construction toys are excellent for developing these skills. Encourage your child to sort items in different ways. He will probably do this naturally! Have you noticed him sorting his toys according to colour, shape or size?

Sorting activities

- Ask your child to sort out all his blue cars while you sort the red ones.
- Sort out different types of pasta into colours and shapes, and make pictures and patterns.
- Give him a tub of coins to sort into different piles.
- Ask him to sort the clean socks into matching pairs, the garden tools into boxes, or the cutlery and plates as you tidy the kitchen.
- Give her buttons, sequins or beads to sort. They could be used to make a picture or a necklace.

Money

Encourage your child to recognise and count coins. Ask him to help when you are giving bus fares or dinner money to older children. When you go on a bus or visit the shops, allow him to count out the fare or the money for the shopping. Remember to let him help you check that you have the right change. And, of course, pocket money encourages children's money skills!

Did you know that one in five adults can't work out the change from £5 after buying a few simple things, according to a Government report in 2000?

Time

Young children soon get a sense of time: time for playschool, lunchtime, bathtime, bedtime and so on. At around five or six years old, children start learning to tell the time in hours, then half-hours, quarter hours and minutes.

Talk aloud as you plan the day, and tell your child how long you expect things to take. For example, tell him, 'We're going to watch Andy play football after lunch. We need to be there at two o'clock. The match will last an hour, so it will finish at three o'clock.' Involve him in decision-making if he is old enough. For example, you might continue: 'Do you think you'll enjoy watching for an hour, or should we leave at half-time, at half-past two?'

When you bake a cake or set the video recorder, work out the times aloud. Involve your child: 'The programme starts at four o'clock. It lasts quarter of an hour, so what time should I set the recorder to finish?'

Half-time is in five minutes. Shall we go home then?

HOME 0
AWAY 0

PAUSE FOR THOUGHT: Using the TV and computer
Many TV programmes and software packages help develop maths skills through fun activities. Simply using a keyboard will help your child learn to recognise numbers and their sequence.

QUICK CHECK
- ✓ Think about choosing different kinds of books for your child.
- ✓ Remember what to do, and not to do, to encourage reading.
- ✓ Know how to make reading fun.
- ✓ Learn what to do to encourage writing.
- ✓ Remember the four rules of number and how to introduce them.
- ✓ Remember that simply talking aloud as you do daily activities helps to develop your child's maths skills.

9

Beyond the School Gates

Getting the best out of your child's school

Have you ever wondered...

? About the differences between learning at school and learning at home?

? How you can help your child cope with her first school?

? How you can help with homework?

? What you can do to prepare your child for tests?

Trying some of the ideas in this chapter will help you explore these issues.

Education works best when it's a genuine partnership between the home and the school. This chapter suggests some ways of helping to make this happen.

? Did you know that schools have, by law, to establish a home/school agreement with parents and children?

WHAT IS YOUR CHILD'S SCHOOL LIKE?

	Yes	No
1. Do you get regular information about what your child is learning?............		
2. Did the school help you prepare your child for school?...............................		
3. Do you get information about how your child is doing?................................		
4. Does the school appear to be a welcoming and friendly place?..................		
5. Does your child get regular homework?..		
6. Is the purpose of the homework clear?...		
7. Have you been invited into your child's classroom to help?.......................		
8. Does your child bring any kind of contact diary home?.............................		
9. Is there an active parents' group?..		
10. Is there somewhere for you to wait when collecting your child?................		
11. Does your child feel able to talk to her teacher?.....................................		
12. Do you feel able to talk to your child's teacher?.....................................		
13. Can you speak to the headteacher easily?...		
14. Are you told when your child does well?..		
15. Do you know what the school's rewards and punishments are?..................		

In an ideal world, you should be able to answer 'yes' to all of these questions. But don't worry if you can't! There are things you can do to help your child get the most out of school.

The ten most important words in the English language are: 'If it is to be, it is up to me!'

Preparing for School

You can make your child's transition to school easier by being aware of the differences between learning at home and at school, and supporting her in coping with these changes. **W** Here are six points you can help her with.

1 Paying attention

Your child will have to follow instructions and stay focused on her teacher, following information on a board or in books. Prepare her for this by giving instructions in a clear voice, one at a time. Get her to say in her own words what you have asked her to do. You can have fun with this by playing 'What did I say?'. You say something and your child repeats it. She then turns her back and you say something else, which she tries to repeat without having seen you. Any games that involve following instructions or explaining the rules to someone else will help.

Practise using questions that make your child think, such as: 'Is that a good idea?', 'What do you think?' or 'Can you say that to me again?'. Teach her to use this sequence when responding to questions: stop, listen, think, reply.

What do you think of my new hairstyle, Nadine?

2 Different physical demands

You can help prepare your child for the physical demands of a classroom by making sure she is used to sitting still for short periods. You might practise by using a kitchen timer while she sits at the table to do something – 5 minutes is about right to begin with.

Practise 'good listening.'

3 Level of noise

Classrooms can be noisy! Help your child realise that sometimes we do things better by being quiet and still. When all the children in a class are good listeners, the class can learn better. Practise 'good listening' with your child: look at the person speaking, keep your hands and feet still, hear what is said and think quietly about it.

4 Purpose of activity unclear

Try to make sure your child knows that it's OK to ask questions if she is unclear about an activity. She needs to be able to get the big picture before she can start working and her teacher may not always manage to make the purpose of a lesson clear.

Is this what I'm meant to wear?

Tips for asking for help

● Ask someone nearby.
● Take a deep breath, put your hand up and say, 'I'm sorry, I didn't understand.... Please can you go over it again?'
● Pretend you didn't hear properly and ask for it to be explained again!

5 Strange routines

Your child will have to respond to bells, form queues and take turns. She will have to sit and work closely with other children, even those she may not like or trust. This strangeness can cause anxiety, which leads to stress. Stress, as chapter 3 shows, can lead to under-performance. Talk to her about school routines and be reassuring. Maybe she has a friend who is already enjoying school and can tell her what it's like. Her anxieties will disappear as she gets used to school.

Mr and Mrs Liang and Winnie, it's lovely to meet you!

6 Unfamiliar adults

Your child will have to learn to respond to adults she hasn't met before. Use opportunities such as open evenings to get to know her teacher. When you talk about her teacher do so positively. Making comparisons between teachers is inevitable but can be unhelpful. Allow your child space to develop her own feelings about her teacher.

For some children, the transition from home to school every morning is a difficult one. To help with this, try to meet a friend outside the school gate, or make the journey to school together.

Supporting Your Child at School

Most primary schools find ways of involving you if you are interested. You might hear children read, go on school trips or help in the library. You might also help to run parents' activities for the PTA (Parent/Teacher Association). There are two key areas of school life that most parents want to help with – homework and tests. Here are some ideas for how best to help your child.

Helping with homework

Your child's school has a 'contract' to provide a certain quality of experience. In turn, you have a contract to provide support for your child's schooling. You can do this by:

1. Creating 'A' time. 'A' time is when homework becomes a priority and your child is given time and space to work quietly and without disruption.
2. Establishing habits around 'A' time. For example, meals should come immediately before 'A' time. Allow your child one hour's play after 'A' time.
3. Avoiding competing activities during 'A' time. For example, others in the family sharing an activity while your child works on her own.
4. Finding a physical space where homework can be done comfortably, with the minimum of disruption.
5. Making the experience pleasurable – providing drinks, good lighting and a warm space.
6. Making sure that the things your child needs are to hand, so she will not have any reason to join you in the living room, for example.
7. Going through homework with your child before and after, and being close by to help with any problems.

Preparing for tests

Children have certain formal tests at school. In the early years, it is the school's job to make these tests so much a part of ordinary lessons that children hardly notice them. Once your child is about 7 years old, you can begin to help her to be ready for tests, and for home study more generally, by suggesting the following approaches.

1. Have the end in mind. Decide what you will achieve by studying. Write this down on a piece of paper or card and put it where you can see it.
2. Get the big picture. Look over your books, notes and other information first. Make sure you have all the things you need nearby.
3. Plan the time. Work out how much time you will spend in total, then break it down into 20 minute chunks.
4. Start it. Once you know what you want to achieve, have sorted what you need, got an overview of the information and planned your time – start!
5. Do it a bit at a time. At the end of each chunk, review what you have done and have a five minute break. Before you begin the next chunk, go over what you are going to do.
6. Draft and re-draft your notes or any written work. Try using a different colour or type of paper for drafts, or make a mind map™ or poster.
7. Self test. At the end of any study session, always test yourself, to see what you can remember.
8. Rehearse. If your test involves writing a timed essay, try it at home first.
9. Build in reward. Reward yourself when you've done what you planned.

QUICK CHECK

✓ Think about ways you can help your child prepare for school.
✓ Remember how you can help with homework.
✓ Learn what to do to prepare your child for tests.

Resources

Games for Learning

Here are a few suggestions for games that will stretch your child's brain (and body). All are fun for adults as well as children. If you want more ideas, ask your local library or bookshop to recommend books of games. Games are often handed down in families, so ask other parents, too.

Categories *2 or more players, age 7+*
This word game is good for learning the alphabet and improving spelling.

Give each player a piece of paper and a pencil. Get them to write the 26 letters of the alphabet down the left-hand side of the paper. You then call out categories of things such as popstars, football clubs, cities, colours, school friends, and even 'things small enough to put in your pocket'. For each category, each player has to think of an example that starts with one of the letters. The aim is to fill in all 26 spaces. This can be very hard!

Coffeepot *3 or more players, age 8+*
This is a guessing game that is good for learning about verbs and sentences.

One player chooses a verb (for example, kick). The rest try to guess what it is by asking questions with the word 'coffeepot' instead of the verb. For example: 'Can anyone coffeepot?', 'Would I coffeepot in the car?' Whoever guesses correctly chooses the next verb.

Famous people *3 or more, age 6+*
This guessing game is good for learning persistence and building confidence.

Take it in turns to think of a famous person. The other players have to guess who you are. You can give them a clue using words or a gesture – either say a catch-phrase or imitate a gesture associated with your famous person. The others have to guess until they get it right or give in.

Cows and bulls *3 or more players, age 9+*
This is a guessing game. It's good for understanding spelling patterns, developing short-term memory and encouraging persistent behaviour.

One player thinks of a four-letter word and the others try to guess it. If they guess the right letter in the right place, the player says 'one bull'. If they get the right letter but in the wrong place, the player says 'one cow'.

So, if the word is ROAD and someone guesses BOAT you would say 'two bulls'. If they guessed DEEP you would say 'one cow', and so on until they guess the word correctly. The game sounds more difficult than it is!

Donkeys and cats *4 or more players (best with more than 6), age 6+*
This is a searching game, which can be played indoors or outside. It's good for developing teamwork, listening skills and quick thinking.

You need two teams, each with one 'retriever', and as many 'finders' as possible. One team is called Donkeys and the other Cats. Before the game, you need to hide 20 or more bits of 'treasure' (like sweets or small biscuits). The idea is for teams to find as many of these as they can.

Each retriever needs to have a bag to put the sweets in. Retrievers are the only ones who can pick up the sweets. When a finder locates a sweet, she must miaow or bray (neigh) depending on which team she's in – no other sounds are allowed! This summons her team's retriever. It also summons the other team, which leads to all sorts of fun!

Yes/no *3 or more, age 7+*
This is good for learning to use new words and finding out how questions work.

The aim is not to use the words 'yes' or 'no'. One player is in the hot seat and has to answer questions from the others. Each of the others tries to trick her into saying yes or no, by asking questions which seem to demand yes/no answers. Once a player uses yes or no, the next player takes over in the hot seat.

Ghost *3 or more, age 8+*
This is a word game that helps with spelling and creative thinking.

The aim of the game is never to be the one who finishes a word. Players take it in turn to say a letter. Each player must have a word in mind as she adds her letter. Other players can challenge if they suspect she hasn't! A game might go like this:

1st player: B
2nd player: O (thinking 'boat')
3rd player: T (thinking 'bottom')
4th player: T (thinking 'bottom')
1st player: O (thinking 'bottom')
2nd player: R (this player has to risk a challenge!)

Wink murder *5 or more, age 5+*
This is a light-hearted game, good for learning close observation.

First get a pack of cards and select the ace of clubs, the queen of hearts and as many other non-picture cards as there are players. The ace of clubs is the murderer and the queen of hearts is the suicide victim.

Sit round a table and deal the cards face downwards. Each player must keep their card completely secret. The player who receives the murderer card has to 'kill' players one at a time, by winking at her victim without being seen by any others. When you are killed, you have to die as dramatically as possible! The other players have to try and spot who is doing the murdering. The game ends when the murderer has been identified. The suicide victim can die whenever he feels like it and can help to divert attention from the murderer.

Useful Websites

There are many good websites for family learning. A good starting point is to use a search engine, such as Google (www.google.com) or Yahoo (www.yahoo.com). Type in key words, or a phrase such as 'Free educational information for children', and see what comes up. Some websites have clearly highlighted sections for parents, teachers and children.

The Ⓦ symbols in the book (on the pages indicated below) show where you can find useful, relevant information by using the websites listed below.

www.topologika.co.uk gives a list of educational websites with a description of each one. The sites are in two groups: information sites for parents and teachers, and activity sites for children and teachers.
www.mum-online.co.uk gives a selection of practical and fun information sites for mothers and children. 'Sites for Mums' includes sites giving advice on bringing up children and OFSTED reports for UK schools. 'Sites for Kids' includes Lego, Disney, NASA and a literacy website called Nature Grid.

Page 17
Ⓦ **www.learntolearn.org** gives ideas on how your child can become a more effective learner.

Page 25
Ⓦ **www.ukeducationguide.co.uk** gives the best homework sites.

Page 45
Ⓦ **www.bbc.co.uk** is probably the best on-line learning resource of all.

Page 49
Ⓦ **www.campaign-for-learning.org.uk** will tell you more about Family Learning Weekend.

Ⓦ **sparkisland.com** has sections for parents and children, with a wide range of interactive learning activities. The parents' section includes 'Boredom Busters' – an excellent free facility, searching for attractions and special events within 10-50km of your postcode area.

Page 51
Ⓦ **www.24hourmuseum.org.uk** has good interactive sections for children.

Page 89
Ⓦ **www.ngfl.gov.uk** is mainly aimed at teachers, but type 'parents' in the search box for relevant information.